Buffalo Dance

Kentucky Voices

Miss America Kissed Caleb

Billy C. Clark

Famous People I Have Known

Ed McClanahan

Buffalo Dance: The Journey of York

Frank X Walker

THE JOURNEY OF YORK

Frank X Walker

THE UNIVERSITY PRESS OF KENTUCKY

Publication of this volume was made possible in part by a grant
from the National Endowment for the Humanities.

Editorial and Sales Offices: The University Press of Kentucky
663 South Limestone Street, Lexington, Kentucky 40508–4008
www.kentuckypress.com

08 07 06 05 04   5 4 3

Map by Dick Gilbreath

Library of Congress Cataloging-in-Publication Data

Walker, Frank X, 1961-
  Buffalo dance the journey of York / Frank X Walker.
    p. cm.
  ISBN 0-8131-2322-4 (hardcover alk. paper)
  ISBN 0-8131-9088-6 (pbk. alk. paper)
  1. York, ca. 1775-ca. 1815—Poetry. 2. Lewis and Clark Expedition
(1804-1806)—Poetry. 3. West (U.S.)—Discovery and exploration—Poetry.
4. African American men—Poetry. 5. Explorers—Poetry. 6. Slaves—Poetry.
I. Title.
  PS3623.A359B84 2003
  811'.6—dc22   2003020512

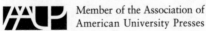

The quadrant, phosphorus, and the magnet were regarded at the Captains' as medicine; that is to say, as supernatural and powerful. The most marvelous was, though, a large, fine man, black as a bear...

—*Pierre Antoine Tabeau, a Missouri River trader who was with the Arikara when the expedition arrived.*

To all the sons and daughters of York who buffalo through the world one word at a time at God's speed, and to my grandson Kenneth D'Juan Sykes. Affrilachian blessings.

Contents

Preface

York, born circa 1772 on a plantation in Caroline County, Virginia spent most of his documented life in Louisville, Kentucky as the body servant of William Clark. He accompanied Clark on the Lewis and Clark Expedition, the Corps of Discovery created by President Thomas Jefferson in 1803 to explore the West and to search for a water route to the Pacific Ocean. After the Louisiana Purchase, which more than doubled the size of the United States, they traveled approximately eight thousand miles in almost three years, returning to St. Louis on September 23, 1806, and Louisville two months later on November 5, after having long been given up for dead.

Both Lewis and Clark kept journals documenting the details of the adventure. Sacagawea's contributions have emerged from beneath the broad shadows of Lewis and Clark's in recent years but York's place has been noticeably absent from the tremendous body of literature surrounding the expedition.

Allowing York's own distinct historical voice and personality to surface while surpressing my own twenty-first century activist voice and ego has been both challenging and humbling. Though silent throughout, I have attempted to be present in the texture and timbre of poem titles and while setting the epigraphs out as guideposts into individual poems. They alone reveal the depth of my own individual passion for a version of "our-story" that can coexist with published historical accounts of this saga.

Feasting on the historical research at night, sleeping, dreaming, and waking with York's version of the journey became the ritual that gave birth to these poems. This journey and York have taught me so much more than any history book or class ever dared. I am honored to have the privilege to serve as a vessel for his voice and for His story. On my best days, I think of myself and the people I love and respect as sons and daughters of York.

The reclamation of mute voices is consistent with the literary contributions and mission of the Affrilachian Poets. What follows are the fictitious observations, thoughts, feelings, dreams, visions, and words of York. His breathing these poems forever establishes him as the original Affrilachian Poet and reinforces the importance and power of the written and spoken Word.

Frank X Walker

Louisville, Kentucky

2003

Acknowledgments

Special thanks to Gurney Norman and Nyoka Hawkins for encouragement; Hasan Davis and Ed Hamilton for introducing me to York; Kathy for the time and space to write; Greg Pape for direction; James Holmberg, Nikky Finney, Ricardo Nazario-Colón, Jim Hall, Mary Ann Taylor-Hall, and Pam Steele for their feedback; Crystal Wilkinson for her motivational speeches; The University Press of Kentucky, Spalding University, and The Filson Historical Society for support; and Faith for her faith and for listening.

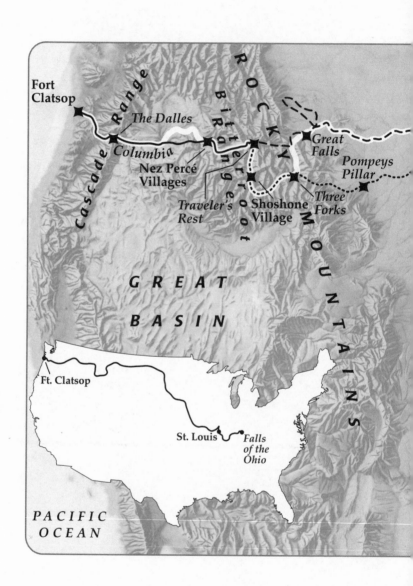

Fort
Clatsop

Cascade Range

The Dalles

Columbia

Nez Percé
Villages

Traveler's
Rest

ROCKY

Bitterroot Range

Bitterroot

M O U N T A I N S

Great
Falls

Pompeys
Pillar

Shoshone
Village

Three
Forks

G R E A T

B A S I N

Ft. Clatsop

St. Louis

Falls
of the
Ohio

PACIFIC
OCEAN

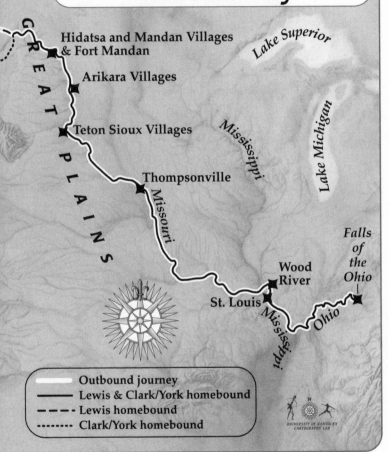

Lewis and Clark Expedition
York's Journey

GREAT

Hidatsa and Mandan Villages
& Fort Mandan

Lake Superior

Arikara Villages

PLAINS

Teton Sioux Villages

Mississippi

Lake Michigan

Thompsonville

Missouri

Falls
of
the
Ohio

Wood
River

St. Louis

Ohio

Mississippi

Outbound journey
Lewis & Clark/York homebound
Lewis homebound
Clark/York homebound

UNIVERSITY OF KENTUCKY
CARTOGRAPHY LAB

Wind Talker

Wind Talker

> Ocian in view! O! the joy.
> —*William Clark*

If I could make my words
dress they naked selves in blackberry juice
lay down on a piece a bark, sheep
or onion skin, like Massa do

If I could send a letter home to my wife
float it in the wind, on wings or water

I'd tell her 'bout Katonka
an all the wide an high places
this side a the big river.
How his family, numbering three
for every star in the sky
look like a forest when they graze together
turn into the muddy M'soura
when they thunder along, faster than any horse
making the grass lay down
long after the quiet has returned.
How they don't so much as raise a tail
when I come 'round with my wooly head
an tobacco skin, like I'm one a them
making the Arikara an Mandan think me
"Big Medicine"
Katonka, who walk like man.

Today, we stood on the edge a all this
looked out at so much water
the mountains we crossed to get here
seem a little smaller.

As I watch fish the size a cabins dance in the air
an splash back in the water like chil'ren playing
I think 'bout her an if we gone ever be free
then I close my eyes an pray
that I don't live long enough
to see Massa make this ugly too.

Work Ethic

Work Ethic

I was deeded to Massa Clark
down on the plantation in Virginy
when he was just a green sapling.
I was less in years but already in a man's body
'cause a all the hard work 'round the place.
We wadn't never what you calls friends
but we pieced together a bond that served us well
for most our time together.

The way it seem to me, the slave only got two choices.
The first is to make up his mind to wake up every day
a slave or steal away in the wind an the night.
An even if the lot he draws is to pick cotton
every day he breathe
he can decide to be the best picker ever was
or fill the bottom a his burlap with rocks an dirt.

I got a better taste a life on the frontier
in Kentucke an the Indian territory
an come to accept my duties as his servant.
It seem like God make my heart even bigger
then the chest it beat in, so I figures
the least I can do is to never let my spirit
be broken by the lash.

A slave needs plenty a fear to survive in Virginy.
I was better suited for the wild, as I had none.

God's House

God's House

> The expedition left the Louisville, Kentucky, area
> near the Falls of the Ohio on October 26, 1803.

When we first left Kentucke
the trees had commenced to dressing up
the fall harvest an the garden
was already full a pumpkins an squash.

Massa Clark didn't ask me to go on no expedition.
He just say "pack" an pointed to the door.
So I gather up what little I got an more than I can carry a his
an head off to a sail-bearing keelboat
where his friend Massa Lewis is waiting.
That boat was so big
you could lay any ten a the sixteen men on board
or eight a me head to toe an still have enough
room for the dog.

We start out on the Ohio an swing up the old man a rivers.
When we gets to the mouth a the dark woman
they calls the Big Muddy
we sets up winter camp a good canoe ride from Saint Louie.

That spring when the rains come we cross the Misssissippi
an commence to climbing the M'soura
an float right up through heaven on earth
more sky than I ever seen, rocks as pretty as trees
an game so plentiful they come right down to the river bank
an invites they selves to dinner.

Now, I ain't what you would call
a scripture quoter, but the first time
I seen the water fall at M'soura,
felt a herd a buffalo stampede
an looked down from top
a Rock Mountains, it was like church.

An where else but God's house can a body servant
big as me, carry a rifle, hatchet ana bone handle knife
so sharp it can peel the black off a lump a coal
an the white man
still close his eyes an feel safe, at night?

Primer

Primer

> I was never so surprised in my whole life as when [on the Middle Passage] I saw the book talk to my master. . . .When nobody saw, I open'd it an put my ear down close upon it, in great hope that it would say something to me.
>
> —*Olauda Equiano, slave*

The only book we 'lowed to know
is the bible, though many a slave
been sold south, had fingers chopped off
an worse
for the crime a reading an writing.

I figures my respect for a good telling
come from listening to Old York
weave his magic at night.
Folk hung from our porch like baby possums
an lived off the breath
he give to every story, no matter how many times
they tasted the tale.

I learn to 'preciate the power a single words
holding the lamp over Massa Clark
while he studied his brother's letters
an struggled with his own returns.

Them think all slaves dumb
'cause we can't cipher, but they be surprised
how many words we pick up
just standing 'round like trees
in a room full a "edjacated" men.

At Ease

Camp Dubois, Winter 1803

The first winter up the Wood River
I learn that being one a massa's soldiers
is a little like being a slave.

After the fort was built, from trees an sweat
the sergeants walked the men back an forth every day.
The privates was made to stand as stiff as oaks
an dance together in straight lines with no music
while they carried they long rifles
like it a parade for the squirrels an the snow.

When I hear tell a the punishment
for sleeping on guard or running off
it make the scars on my back itch a little.

Sundays and Christmas

Sundays and Christmas

Because of York's duties as Clark's traveling full-time
body servant and the fact that his wife was owned by
another family in Louisville, they lived apart and saw
each other infrequently.

I cares plenty for my wife
but I been told a slave can't truly know love
being as Massa an white mens in general
have an takes certain privileges with our women.

I suspect the deepest hurt in the world
be to risk being tied to a woman's hearth
then standing on the front porch
while the massa part her thighs
knowing that any cry raised
is inviting death or worse.

But what else but love
make you hold that woman even tighter
try to rock her back to whole
long after the tears dry up
an the hurt
turns the ashes
back to flames.

It being night time an deep into winter
I can think a no other breath I wish to feel
an no other whisper I ache to hear.
What we 'lowed to feel might not rate as love
but it be powerful enough to make
you rue the time between visits.

Calendar

May 1804

While at the first winter fort
I 'most run outa fingers
counting how many moons
we been gone from old Kentucke.

Watched the trees give
all they leaves to the ground
to make a bed for the snow
an winter put the bears hard to sleep.

I seen man-sized drifts finally melt to nothing
spring rains green an flower the ground
an bring the goose an every little thing
with wings back home.

Seen the creeks fill they selves back up
with fish, an us roasting dinner
head an all beneath trees
already dressed up again for courting.

When we gets more than a week up the M'soura
from the Mississippi, it seem like
we just float off
yesterday.

Her Current

Working up stream against the current
be like courting a stubborn woman.
We spend the whole day trying to make a little distance
an her attitude don't change a bit.

If we don't seem to notice that she be thicker
at some points than others or how deep she can get
she punish us all an run the boats aground.
An just when we 'bout to give up
she feed us, bathe us an rocks us to sleep.

Capt. Lewis seem to think that if we puts up with her
long enough, like all women
she gone change her mind
an carry us along so fast
it likely to take us breath away
when she welcomes us with arms
as wide as an ochian.

Medicine Men

> Sergeant Floyd is taken very bad all at once with a
> bilious colic. . . . He gets worse and we are much
> alarmed at his situation.
>
> —*William Clark, August 19, 1804*

Capt. Lewis attended to the party's doctoring
by dispensing his fix-all, the Doctah's Thunderbolt
that sent the men scurrying to the bushes for relief
complaining that they emptied them whole insides
on the ground an left they backsides raw
from so much good health.

He pass out a salve to them whose privates be
itching an peeling from so much
spilling them wild oats
at some a the villages along the way.

It was me that was called to attend to Sgt. Floyd
before he died an Sacagawea the last moon
before her child come.
Capt. Clark must have let on
that I picked up a thing or two 'bout roots an wild grasses
from Old York an his Rose.

Before the Sgt. turn loose his last breath
he refused the twenty-third psalm an prayer
an asked my Capt. to write him a letter.

When Massa read his long list a apologies an regrets
out loud, they hung in the air
like eagles.

Spirit Mound

> We returned to the boat at sunset, my servent nearly
> exosted with heat thurst and fatigue, he being fat and
> unaccustomed to walk as fast as I went was the cause.
> —*William Clark, August 25, 1804*

Capts. Clark an Lewis together with nine mens
an me along to carry an cook
walked 'most a whole day to see Spirit Mound.

I didn't want to go no place
so sacred even the Indians afraid to step,
so I pretends to be more tired than I was.

This piece a land so full a spirits
I felt little hairs praising on the back a my neck
but Capt. Clark don't seem to understand
what be sacred to others any more
than he see the difference
tween me ana pack mule.

Maybe the chief should have bade him
to think a it as the Great White Father's
mother's undergarments or that
what's under her skirt.

Wasicum Sapa

Wasicum Sapa*

Several mile up the river Capt. Clark
named after a tribe a the Sioux
a Hidatsa chief sent for us.
His eagle feather & pride
made him 'most as tall as me

He spit on his fingers
an rubbed my skin hard,
thinking it paint that wears off.
Meaning to help
him understand, I took off my hat
an let him touch my wooly head.

Satisfied that I was not
a black white man
he looked deep into my eyes
an stared at his own reflection.

*Black man in the Sioux language

Winter Leaf

Fort Mandan, October 24, 1804

After the three days a tight fists, rooster strutting
an sour stomachs spent with Sioux
Capt. Clark called the "pirates a the M'soura"
an some other harsh names
we was so pleased to meet the warm Mandan
that we raised our second winter fort
across the river from they great town a earth houses.

My blackness was greeted with great respect
an the chil'ren followed me so close they
become a part a my shadow.

On cold nights when we shared camp fires, stories
an music, Massa ordered me to dance
which they enjoyed greatly, as much for my skill
an quick feet, as they surprise to see a oak tree
move as nimble as a leaf.

Buffalo Dance

Buffalo Dance

Mandan Village, January 5, 1805

For several long nights filled with drums an whistles
young men leaped an circled 'round the fire
dressed in whole heads an horns, some in tails
all singing for the return a Katonka
an begging seasoned warriors to gift them
with they courage an hunting skills
by passing it through they favorite wives.

The fire danced too
but mostly with shadows a women
standing tall an quiet, naked beneath buffalo robes.
The heat an dancing made hindquarters an faces shine
like pack horses a mile into a full trot.

The young warriors moved with
the grit an pluck ova runaway slave
an paid no never mind to tired bodies an feet
as if pressed on by ghost hounds in the distance.

If the old men returned to the circle
with wives who had not been used
they would be offered again an again
with even more wailing an begging
'til the only drums beating was us hearts.

I was among the unbelievers
'til the buffalo come just four days later
an well-horsed warriors took many many more
with bows an arrows
than we could with all our guns.

No Offense

Ol' drinking gourd
you my witness tonight
an you don't have to holler back
moan or amen none neither
just keep on shining, an blinking
an listening.

Now, I ain't a perfect man.
Don't reckon I know none
black or white,
but I don't know how
to bring offense to a man
who ask me to his lodge
an leave one a his wives to pleasure me
while he stand guard
out front.

Capt. Clark an his men say it wrong,
but them say nothing
when they stumbles drunk
to the slave quarters, back in Kentucke
an have they way
with any girl child or woman
they find, whether she be married
or not.

Them want me to be shamed
but I can't find fault
with a man who think so much a me
he want his wife to hold my seed.

Leading Men

Leading Men

Sacagawea and her husband a French Canadian inter-
preter and trader living with the Hidatsas joined the
expedition in North Dakota, April 1805

When we left the Mandan village
an the river
Touissant's squaw, the dog
an me was in back, dragging more than
our share a the load
then we gets so far out in the wild
the men's military voices an steps
lose all they thunder an air.

After some commence to walking on they toes,
mistaking tree roots for rattlers an wasting
precious ball an powder on shadows an the wind
Capt. Clark puts us an the nine young men
from Kentucke out front.

I gets taller
the dog gets to run
an Sacagawea just smiles an nods.

Domestique

Domestique[*]

I picks up a few Shoshoni words an signs
from the foreign man's squaw.
She point to the men an say "daiboo"
an then at me an say "duu daiboo"
I figures the duu is for my blackness
after I sees her rub her cheek.

It seem like her Frenchman speak to her
through his nose sometimes.
His tongue got more flowers on it
than Capt. Clark's, but fetch my supper,
make my bed an bend over
sound the same in any language.

*"Servant" in the French language

Work Song

Me an Sacagawea
cook an carry water
an fire wood before we
starts the days an long
after we stop to rest our aching feet.

She tip toe 'round
with a song in her mouth
like my people do back
in Kentucke with her little brave
tied to her back

They think we just happy
to do the work
but singing songs an laughing a little
somehow makes the load lighter
an keeps the bitter taste
from crawling out our throats
an sitting on our tongues
ready to strike.

Perfume

I must have the ache
for my own wife tonight
'cause I swear
when I raise my head
I can smell Sacagawea
suckling her new cub
an there be
a smokey wood fire
a party a musky mens
ana warm breeze off the river
between us.

Black Magic

When we broke winter camp an headed deeper
into the wild in
search a the Shoshoni,
Sacagawea's new son was still suckling.

Taken away in a raid when just a girl,
sold to Touissant who then married her
she turn out to be the sister a the chief
in charge a the horses Massa mean to trade
a bunch a nothing for
in order to cross
the mountains squinting at us
from where the sky an land meet.

Men in the party believes we's lucky
but I seen our boats hit rocks an not split open,
rattlers under foot an not strike.
I seen a buffalo charge into camp an not trample
a single sleeping man.

Capt. Lewis think he smart
believe his power come from Washington
but I suspect that something bigger
got they hand in this.
Something familiar as the night sky
an more dependable than the ground under our feet.

Sandstone Thighs

Sandstone Thighs

the hills & river cliffs which we passed today exhibit
a most romantic appearance...They are formed of re-
markable white sandstone....
> —*Meriwether Lewis, May 31, 1805*

After many campfire talks between lonely men
'bout who seen the best parts a the most
beautiful gals, the argument was settled
when we float by tall wide cliffs
so soft on the eyes it cause all the men
to whistle, shout an carry on
like we was passing a porch full
a bare-legged women
showing off a little more than thigh.

Knowing my place, I sneaks a few glances
over my shoulder an stare at the pretty
white legs in the face a the river.

Mouths and Waters

Mouths and Waters

...the grandest sight I ever beheld...the rocks below
receiving the water in its passage down and breaks it
into a perfect white foam which assumes a thousand
forms in a moment.
    —*Meriwether Lewis, June 13, 1805*

The beauty a the sandstone thighs
stayed with the party 'til we reached
the falls a the M'soura.
The laughing an singing in the distance
grew louder the closer we came.
When we finally feast us eyes on a wide wet woman
dancing an leaping with joy off the rocks
an raining down her own rainbow,
our mouths fall open
an we commence to dance an shout
like a field fulla colored chil'ren d'scovering
tobacco leaves made a gold
an sweat be sweet as honey.

The Portage

The party was confronted with five falls over a ten-mile
stretch of the river, meaning a portage of over eigh-
teen miles. A month passed before they were able to
put their boats into navigable water again. June 16-
July 14, 1805

The spell a the river's beauty wear off
after it become too dangerous to stay in the water.
So we picks up the whole camp, boats an all
an stumble an carry everything a good many miles
'round the great falls, her sisters an all they sharp rocks.

When it gets rough, I hear Old York remind me
that like teeth on a rose, pretty girls is nothing but trouble.
Then his Rose jump in an say she wish she were a yard bird
'cause even the rooster know when it time to shut up.

As I stop to rest an laugh, it come to me
that every soft an pretty thing God make
got a hard an ugly to carry with it.

Sun Son

Sun Son

While enjoying the feel a the day on my face
it come to me that a good hat ought to serve
a man in at least three ways
keep him head warm when it cold
keep it dry when the clouds open up
an provide a little comfort for his eyes
when there be nothing but sun in the sky.

The men complain that the sun
might not make mischief like the wind
but it drink the water out ova man
as easy as it sit on the ground in the morning.

Them with skin 'most like flour seem to suffer an peel
more than others, but the sky king seem to like
my shiny black self 'most as much as the mosquita.

Double Yolks

They wasn't what you call opposites
in the way that salt is to pepper
or night is to day.
But they was a natural team, yoked
together the way hands an feet
work out they differences in order
to pick up a thing an carry it to some other place.

To have one a them drown or to pass on
like Sgt. Floyd did a spell back
would a been like paddling a canoe
only on one side.

Capt. Clark had some book learning
but Massa Lewis held on to the things he read
the way a boy swoon forever 'bout his first kiss.
He pull sayings out the air like he plucking fruit
then smile 'cause he like the way it taste.
He had a bucket full a two-dollar words
he used when scratching in his books.
He scribble for hours 'bout one little flower
or strange new animals like the deer-goat
an the little toy dogs we come 'cross
that lived in holes in the ground.

Capt. Clark, at home on or off the river
might scratch in his book for a minute, but he seem to prefer
the company 'round the fire
where he laughed an talked an defended
his friend's long walks an time alone with his dog an books.

Two roosters could never be friends in a barnyard
but these two took turns crowing an giving orders
an was so often a the same mind you would think
they was hatched from the same egg.

What seem to bind them together was not just
orders from Washington but the cocksure notion
that they would finish what they started
or die trying, together.

Ornithologists

Ornithologists

> Several new species collected during the expedition
> were named after Lewis and Clark, including Lewis's
> woodpecker (*Melanerpes lewis*) and Clark's crow
> (*Nucifraga columbiana*).

We picked up a few things
watching the Indians track an hunt.
They know the calls an movements
a birds an animals
so much so, they can mock anything
in the woods, even deer
an them don't hardly speak.

The Captains have us all looking an listening
for birds an beasts an was happy as larks
if we could bring something new with wings
back to camp, mostly whole or breathing.

Capt. Lewis would peer into his eyeglass stick for hours
trying to know a bird that caught his eye
an could scratch out on paper exactly how the thing be.
Shape a the head an beak, markings on the feathers,
toes, feet, an all.

It was like the woodpecker or crow an such
just walk up, make itself small
an lay right down on the page.

Swap Meet

The Indian Peace Medals produced for Thomas
Jefferson's administration began the series of round
medals bearing the image of the president. The re-
verse side featured clasped hands of friendship, a
crossed tomahawk and peace pipe, and the bold in-
scription, PEACE AND FRIENDSHIP.

After parading the uniformed men
an guns an other signs a power
the Capts. sat with each Chief
made great noise 'bout peace an friendship
before heaping upon them gifts a knives, tobacco
spirits, needles, cloth an beads a every size an color
which pleased the women very much.

Calling them "chil'ren"
The Capts. would point to everything under the sky
say it now belong to their Great White Father
an show off his image on the face side ova big coin
they unwrapped an presented with much putting on.

Sometimes the Chiefs would laugh
an say the Great Spirit who own all this
could not ride on the back a such a small thing.

Sometimes them say nothing.

Promises

Promises

> It does not require many words to speak the truth.
> —*Chief Joseph, Nez Perce*

Many tribes speak they piece
by talking with they hands an faces.
When we sit in the circle to talk
with Sacagawea's brother, the chief
she take his words in Shoshoni
an measure them out in Hidatsa
Charbono hands it to Lebiche in French
Lebiche gives it to the Captains in English
then they talks between themselves
an sends it back down the line
an so forth an so on.

The words seem to be on they own expedition
but it hard to believe the truth
can be traded on that many tongues
an still taste like itself.

Nomenclature

Nomenclature

> Some of the party with him told the Indians that we
> had a man with us who was black and had short curl-
> ing hair, this had excited their curiosity very much,
> and they seemed quite anxious to see this monster as
> they were the merchandize which we had to barter
> for their horses.
>> —*Meriwether Lewis*

All my life I been told
that my big nose an wooly hair
was ugly beastly things
an the closer to black a person is
the more mule he be.
So there be none more mule than me.

In the Indian world my blackness
is a thing to be worshipped,
my nose a sign a power.

Capt. Clark call these beautiful
an kind peoples "ignorant savages."
But it don't take a edjacated man
to guess what they think
a his thin nose an pale face.

Respect House

Respect House

Inside a teepee be round an perfect
as the sun or the new moon itself.
Buffalo skins hug the pine frames pointing
an stretching to the sky in such a way
it remind even a small man to bow
his head an stay close to the earth.

When the Shoshoni, follow the herd
across the great grass on hunting parties
they travel with they pine an skin moons
tied to the back a dogs or horses.

Unless we build a winter fort
I sleeps on the cold hard ground
under the open sky dreaming
a waking on piles a buffalo robes
inside a house a respect.

Prosperity

I love the land and the buffalo and will not part with it...
Satanta, Kiowa Chief

The summer after the second winter
with the Mandan
when I sees how much use them all gets
from the buffalo, wasting nothing
it put me in mind a my people
an how well them get to know the pig
after massa carry off the hams an shoulders
to eat for himself.

Out back in the quarters in Virginy an Kentucke
we makes a feast out a that what's left. We eats
the tongue, feet, skin, innards an even give thanks
for the pleasure ova pig ear sandwich,
but where the slave barely survive off leftover swine
the red man live good off the buffalo.

Vision Quest

At midnight may I roam against the winds...May I
roam when the owl is hooting. May I roam when the
crow is calling...

—*Teton Sioux song, translated
by Frances Densmore*

Last night, I dreamed that the old woman came to me
an offered me a gift a tobacco tied to an eagle feather.
After puffing the sacred pipe in my left hand
while fanning the smoke over my head with my free hand
I walked out a the lodge an rolled on the ground
in the high grass.
When I got up I was a buffalo
an the old woman was singing.

When she stopped her song she took a long pull a water
an spit it in the four directions an bade me look behind me.
Old York, his Rose, my wife an all the slaves I knowed
back in Virginy an Kentucke was rolling 'round on the ground
turning themselves into a small herd.

When I turned back to where the old woman was sitting
she was holding a bowl a water an bade me look into it.
All I saw was her smiling face an a giant Crow
staring back at me.
Then as a strong wind came an carried me off
I hollas back to the herd an say
"One day I will return an bring all a you wings."

Vision Quest II

Vision Quest II

Today I dream that
I floats so high the morning fog
that help break the day along the river
look like a giant cloud snake
hugging the ground
winding itself through the hills an valleys.

Then the snake split in two
then three, then a whole family
is stretched full out amongst
the rocks an trees

By an by I gets so high
the Rock Mountains is play stones
an the great plains, just a country acre.
Directly the fog burn off
an turn the snakes into a looking glass.

I gets higher still
'til I can see both ochians.
An all the rivers sit on the land
like silver horns on a bull.

On the way back down to my body
I float over a storm cloud
heading east like a runaway bull
lighting itself up as it go.

When I make to stare at it
it put me in mind
ova buffalo Jesus, wooly,
angry, an full a the revelations.

Ananse

Ananse*

When spring come
the Mandan, Arikara an Hidatsa gather 'round the fire
sing, dance an tells they in-the-beginning stories.
Stories so full they puts
that tale from Genesis to shame.

Old York say we come from clay
but that I first sprung out the ground
'most full grown, then laugh.

The Indians, them say they climbed up out the ground
one by one
until a pregnant woman's weight
broke the vine
creating the living an the dead
or tunneled through the dirt like the badger or mole
while still animals
helping the Corn Mother
who not only gave them food an wisdom
but brought Nishanu out the sky
to teach them to make war
on their enemies.

I try to keep every word I hear alive in my head
so I can carry them back an warm the fires at home.
I thinks my people will 'preciate stories where
whoever struggle in the beginning
make out alright in the end.

> *Ananse is the spider, a heroic character in African folklore.
> Like Br'er Fox he outwits all the other creatures of the forest.

Mythology

I catch them whispering on an on 'bout
me an "it" an pretending not to look
when I goes to the river to empty myself.

Once them say, "Boy, was that river cold?"
an commence to laugh hard an mighty between them.
Then I say, "No Sir, but it plenty deep,"
an snort like the horse them think I am.
Then we all laughs an by an by they forget
who got the last lick.

Earth Tones

> the old Lakota was wise. He knew that man's heart,
> away from nature, becomes hard; he knew that lack
> of respect for growing , living things soon led to lack
> of respect for humans too.
>
> —*Chief Luther Standing Bear, Oglala Sioux*

Massa believe the earth an all her chil'ren
be like wild horses that need to be broke
saddled, counted, owned, renamed, corralled
an made to serve.

Most Indian peoples we come across
seem to be partners with the land,
the water an all things that have breath
or reach for the sun.

When I sits by the river at night
listening to the darkness breathe
the hoot owl say,
Who say they own the land?
Who say they own her chil'ren?
Who? Who?

After I answers, I pours out some spirits
an ask forgiveness for my role in it
when I see that building fences
an even cleaning Massa's stable
make me just another whip in his hands.

Sweat Lodge

> When the buffalo went away the hearts of my people fell to the ground, and they could not lift them up again. After this nothing happened. There was little singing anywhere.
>
> —*Chief Plenty Coups, Crow*

I seen things in my sleep
that make me afraid
to shut my eyes at night.

A pack a white coyotes
was chasing a herd a buffalo
an killing them one by one,
but they would not feed on the meat.

As far as you could see there was nothing
but flesh rotting in the sun
an the noise from the flies feeding on their deaths
was so great the people did nothing but weep.

The old woman who lives in my dreams
gave me a silver powder horn
an begged me to raise my long rifle
but I was too afraid.

The rain joined her tears
an flooded the rivers red.
When I returned to my self
I was soaked like a sack a oats in a creek bed
but what I thought was blood
was only sweat.

Doubt

Doubt

Passing through the Bitterroot Mountains and along
the ancient Lolo Trail they encountered hazardous
travel and hardship. August 30–September 9, 1805

The onliest time I felt like giving in
was the eleven days an nights we spent
wandering through the bitter peaks
trying to follow an old buffalo trail.

Old man winter, who seem to always
come sooner an stay longer in the mountains
whether he be invited or not
brung so much snow our guide lead us across
our own footstep.

The going was so rough an steep
between climbing over dead trees
an slipping an falling off wet rocks
the horses, with four legs, barely keeps they feet,
while us with only two was slowed to a cold wet crawl.

There came a cold spell so mean
it made us bones ache, turned our faith to ice
an some a the men blue.

With game smarter than us an no where
to be found, we fed off three colts
too small to carry a full load,
rather than eats each other or Massa Lewis' dog.

Cold Hearted

Cold Hearted

> My boy york verry unwell from violent colds & strains
> carrying in meet and lifting logs on huts to build them.
> —*William Clark, winter 1805*

After the river change her mind
then turn back on herself
all the rain an snow
keep me full a the hack an the snots.

When we first start out I was
wearing my one pair a sack breeches
an both my long an short shirts
all way too thin for these cold winters
but nothing for a Virginy born slave
to complain 'bout.

Walked holes in my shoes before we reached
the Mandans an come down with the frost
on my feets an my privates
while out hunting with Massa Clark.

Him like the ugly weather
'most as much as he like his warm stockings
long underwear, army boots
an coats a fur.

When he see me shiver he say the slave not made
for the cold. I say old man winter be a harsh massa too.

Sad Eye

Lying here under this big sky
the river singing softly
in the distance put me in mind
a old York's stories a the Gambia.
He don't fret none on it
but it must been a terrible thing
to be snatched up from your own mamma's knees
an herded off to be sold like cattle.

I figures none a the weak survived being made
to ride in the bottom ova boat 'cross the
African Sea, surrounded by death
an shackled in piles a they own filth.

He say I'm lucky to be born in Virginy.
To walk on the same dirt as my mamma.
I suspect he right, but I think the sad eye he get
when he look up at the heavens at night,
put him in mind a when he used to be free.

Some times when it late, he stand in the field
close his eyes an reach up an smile
like he can 'most touch it.

I reckon freedom an Africa be like having
a whole sky to yourself.

Aurora Borealis

Aurora Borealis

> Last night late we wer awoke by the sergeant
> of the Guard to See a northern light...
> —*William Clark*

Between the Captains an Sgt. Gass
somebody scribble 'most every night.
When the pages fill up, the books
be so alive they given names an birth dates.

Sometimes in the deep a the night
the north sky get full a something like writing
only the rows a letters
be long streaks a light
as if even God is writing everything down.

When we come 'cross rock drawings
that seem as old as the stone that wear it,
I wonder for the first time
how I can leave my mark
in the world.

Electorate

Electorate

At the mouth of the Columbia River, an event occurs
that is the first known documented time in American
history that a woman, an Indian, and a black man
voted.—December 1805

North a the big river that bleed into the ochian
Capt. Clark give me a proxy, Sacagawea too
say our words count, then we all have our say
to decide where we gone pitch a fort that winter.

Now I done served him way past good
even before this expedition; risked my own life
searching for him in a powerful storm what blowed up,
swam out to a rocky garden wrestling ice cold current
to pick greens for his digestion,
hunted down an carried back deer, elk an even buffalo
for his supper.

I takes all the power the red man gives to me
on account a my blackness
an place it at my Capt.'s feet
making him more powerful in they eyes.

That winter, he give me my own proxy
say my word count too,
but I knows not to get too full a myself
'cause come dark, I still have to pick the fleas
off his blanket a skins, so at least he sleep
straight through the night.

Winter with Jonah

Fort Clapsop near Astoria, Oregon, winter 1806

In this beautiful ugly place, the winter sky
bring so much more rain than sun
I spent a month a nights praying for one dry day.
It stay so wet, us clothes 'most rot off
an what little meat we try to smoke don't keep
for the damp.

When not hunting elk, we keeps a handful a men
an a fire going on the shore
to boil down pots full a ochian
an collect the salt that hide there.

As if standing next to all that water
an more than forty days an nights a rain
fail to humble the men an make them
ever mindful a the power a God

One a those cabin-size fish washed up on shore
an even have Capt. Clark giving thanks
out loud that the good Lord send us a monster
to swallow rather than be swallowed
like ol' Jonah.

Majesty

From their camp on the Williamette River, the party
could see Mount Rainier, Mount St. Helens, and
Mount Hood. March 1806

From our camp on the river
the Indians call Multnomah
we took our time drinking in the
three kings in the distance.

They seem to rise so high in the sky
they breaks open holes in the clouds
an hold tight to they winter crowns
no matter what the sun say down here.

When buffalo die they souls
must live in these mountains
these rocky hairs on God's own head.

I may not ever see them again
but I means to lock them in my mind
'til I needs more reminding
a how much like the ant we really be.

Pomp's Tower

Pomp's Tower

Summer 1806

With help from the Pierced Nose we survived
the mean an bitter trail again.
We all got much-needed baths an soaks
in the hot water ponds Massa mapped
on the way to the ochian, then we split up
at the creek the Capts. Call Travelers Rest.

The part a us not traveling with Capt. Lewis
made our way to the Yellowstone
where we come across a big tired rock
that looked down on us an even the tallest trees.
It sat all alone in the tall grass
like a wounded buffalo bull
an paid no never mind when Massa
carved his mark in its side.

The Little Sneeze

We pass time near the fire
swapping stories an sharing songs.
Sometimes Capt. Lewis calls up
some a the little sayings he carry 'round
in his head.

They ain't but a breath long an
comes an goes so fast,
I names 'em after the sneeze, the haichu.

They don't stir the men much
so sometimes he leave the fire
in a huff mumbling
something 'bout how useless
it be to dress pigs in silk
which cause the men to choke an tear up
something awful
an finally Massa too.

York Haichu

A still tongue be a good friend
but a helping hand be sweet as a wife.

A quiet woman be better company
than a drunk an ugly man.

Good whiskey will wake a sleeping dog an
drag him howling thru the fire.

The hand all men wipe with, stinks,
unbelievers need only smell they own.

Next to God, only the daylight can be
counted on to tell the truth.

Not all snakes rattle before they bite, or
ever ask what color you be.

The taste a freedom like food,
water, matter most to them who have none.

Pastry Chefs

Pastry Chefs

> The party was introduced to many native foods, including Camas [Camassia quamash]. Weippe Prairie, June 11, 1806

I seen Old York's Rose turn a hand full a yams,
ugly green apples an a plain old pumpkin
into dishes so sweet you believe she kin
to the honeybee. She say a good cook
can always make something out a nothing.

The Nez Perce women prove her right
by harvesting the roots
a plants we first mistake for water
the way they blue flowers covered the field
twinkling like a wet blanket.

Like Capt. Clark, who always request
a special meal come his birthday
I be so partial to these roots
I pretends that today is mine.

I figures a man as black as me
had to be born when the sun scream the loudest.
Few slaves know they exact day
so I claims the whole summer.

My wife an Old Rose would call these women
sisters an cousins, if they could see
what it take to build a room-size fire in the ground
an smoke an cook for half a day
just to get the root sweet an black as me.

Unravel

After the journey, Clark settled in St. Louis and re-
mained in government service until his death in 1838.
Lewis found neither success or happiness upon his
return and committed suicide in 1809.

I reckon the only sour part 'bout pouring
your whole self into a thing
like finding the ochian,
be finding it.

On the trip back home we seem to run
all out a laughter an good will.
We all sunk pretty low, but our hearts
touched the ground when we left Sacagawea
back with the Mandan an Hidatsa.
Her company had been a spark a light for me
when the sun had gone down on everything else.
Her little brave made such a mark on Massa Clark
that he offered to keep him to raise.

There was days when Capt. Lewis hardly opened his mouth
even to Massa Clark. This seemed odd for a man
who loved words so. Tempers was short.
Camp fires was quiet.
The good in some a these men
would lay down with them at night
an be gone by sun up.

It seem like the search for the treasure
was the real treasure. After kissing the ochian
the expedition just become
a long trip home.

Revisionist History

fired three rounds as we approached the shore and
landed oppocit the center of the Town, the people
gathered on the shore...
—*William Clark, September 23, 1806*

When we set foot back in old Saint Louie
there was much celebration an putting on
as everyone had give us up for dead.
We paraded through the streets firing our guns
an made a home in the nearest tavern.
No one seemed to tire a hearing us tell
our stories night after night.

After too many cups an tellers
there came tales a herds a grizzlies,
big talking fish an Indian women ten foot tall.

The truth seemed to stretch so
that by an by I seem to disappear from they tongues
as if I had never even been there
as if my blackness never saved they hides.

Them twist the tales an leave out my parts in it
so much so, that directly I become Massa Clark's boy, again
just along to cook
an carry.

Monticello

1785 Virginia law declares that "every person, who
has one-fourth or more of Negro blood shall be
deemed a mulatto."

I tried to picture a yard full a lil' sun-kissed Yorks
after we stopped at the school in Danville
to see Massa's nephews who was boarded there.

Days later, when we arrived bone tired
in Washington to see the Great White Father,
Massa Clark left me with the servants.

All a Sally's yellow chil'ren had what them call
"good" hair an light eyes
an walked 'round with they noses up
puttin' on airs, claiming to be Jefferson's own.

I wonder if they family pride will still have legs
when they leave this place
an find out that any child born to a slave
is still a slave, no matter how white or high the daddy be.

Plantations is full a truths an whispers
'bout whose daddy is whose.
Old York say babies' noses don't know to lie
an one drop a Africa
be enough to sweeten a lip or curl even the reddest hair.

Souvenir

Souvenir

> promit him to Stay a few weeks with his wife, he
> wishes to Stay there altogether and hire himself which
> I have refused. He prefers being Sold to retun[ing]
> here, ...if any attempt is made by york to run off, or
> refuse to provorm his duty as a slave, I wish him sent
> to New Orleans and Sold, or hired out to Some Se-
> vere master until he thinks better of Such Conduct.
>
> —*William Clark, in a letter to his*
> *brother Jonathan, Nov. 9,1808*

Massa Clark sent his brother several boxes
filled with pelts, horns, moccasins an other
Indian goods received in trade back home,
on the keelboat, from the Mandans.
I sent my wife a buffalo robe
to put her in mind a me when winter come again.

I been carrying some gifts a Indian corn, a seashell
from the ochian, a grizzly bear tooth, an some
rocks rubbed smooth by the M'soura in the medicine bag
I keeps 'round my neck.

Though it been three long winters since I seen
her smile, Massa be so set in his old ways
I fear that next time I sets my eyes on her might be my last.

Just Rewards

Just Rewards

> . . . he has got such a notion about freedom and his
> emence Services, that I do not expect he will be of
> much service to me again...I gave him a severe trounc-
> ing the other Day and he has much mended sence.
> —*William Clark in a letter to Jonathan*
> *Clark, December 10, 1808*

I rowed an walked as much an carried more
than any man on the expedition.
When we returned
Massa Clark got acres a land, lots a pay
an grand balls in his honor.
I got a short week in Kentucke
to say good bye
to my wife before returning to his new home in Saint Louie.

Unable to fill all my emptiness with whiskey
I earned many lashes at his hands
for being what he calls "insolent an sulky"
or what I calls speaking up for my freedom.

A Love Supreme

A Love Supreme

On that first night back
me an her move like turtles
unwrapping the old, the news
an each other.

We out last the candle an the moon
laughing an talking an crying
then pretends we are earth an sky
hunger an fruit, a black mountain
ana all-skin-quilt a snow.

Salty an sticky an wet
we knows all we have
is this here,
so we unshackle us clothes
become one with the night
an be free.

Holy Water

Holy Water

I don't know what get in Massa's head
an have him think a generous whip
make me a better slave.

Don't know who told that lie
'bout whiskey making ugly pretty
or drinking taking pain away.

But what else put a song in your mouth
when there be nothing left
to sing 'bout?

What else let you laugh at the hand full a salt
rubbed deep into your own bloody flesh?
Make you forget how much you hates being alive?

Make you believe you can drown
all your loss, all your fears,
an wash away any thoughts a revenge?

It seem like the life ova slave
is only the first parts a Easter
So, I sprinkle myself, bare my back an swallow.

Ursa Major

Ursa Major

> ...the bear, which was verry large and a turrible look-
> ing animal, which we found verry hard to kill...This
> animal is the largest of the carnivorous kind I ever saw."
> —*William Clark*

When I be my best self, I be all buffalo.
Quiet as a mountain, proud, strong, without fear
able to see the good in everything.

But like most God's creatures
when I can't find my own light
or when the world try to blow it out
there be a darker York. A York that mirrors
more the grizzly then the wooly-headed thunder-bringer.

Knowing how much Massa Clark fear
the Great Bear, after seeing that his bullets
only seem to make him mad;
when I sinks deep into my worst self,
with a little help from whiskey's bite
I try to bring as much fear an destruction
as anything we run upon in the wild.

This grizzly knows no fear an is not afraid to die.
He is only afraid that when he wakes up
he'll just be a slave again.

Cumulonimbus

Cumulonimbus

What I come to know is
no man born a slave.
Serving another, for life
agreeing to be treated like cows
an pigs an less
be something a slave weigh every day
after he look at his other choices,
death an running.

Slaving, ain't no picnic.
We might look happy but
us grin mostly to keeps from crying.

Old York say
it take something African
to stand in the rain an smile
while it storming all 'round.
He say nobody choose to slave.
Them choose to hold on
to what little family them got.
Them choose to be sure
somebody still here to tell our side
to tell the whole truth
when it all said an done.

What some calls lightning an thunder
just be God trying to see what we choosing
an us grumbling
'bout being slaves.

Birth Day

Clark reported that York died alone and miserable in
Tennessee though, it is rumored that he returned to
the west and lived out his days as a chief among the
Crow Indians.

I reckon that made him feel bigger than me,
planting that lie 'bout me dying a the cholera
in Tennessee.
He was part right, but what died wasn't no man.
It was my desire to serve him, to be his boy
after all I done seen an done.

His body servant sure enough passed on, but not below
Kentucke.
Every step to the ochian an back
every winter spent keeping him warm
knocked a little spring out a me.

What he knowed as York, died making his life easy
an was born again, the other side a Rock Mountains,
in the middle ova herd a wooly headed buffalo
breathing mountain air so clean an cold it make
your ears fill up, your head try an float away
your eyes just turn to ochians.

About the Author

Frank X Walker, a founding member of the Affrilachian Poets (the subjects of the award-winning documentary *Coal Black Voices*), is the editor of *Eclipsing a Nappy New Millennium* (Haraka Press), the author of *Affrilachia* (Old Cove Press), and a recipient of an Al Smith Fellowship from the Kentucky Arts Council. His poetry has been converted into a stage production by the University of Kentucky Theatre department and widely anthologized in numerous collections including *The Appalachian Journal, Limestone, A Kentucky Christmas, Roundtable, Wind, My Brother's Keeper, Spirit and Flame: An Anthology of Contemporary African American Poetry,* and *Role Call: A Generational Anthology of Social and Political Black Literature and Art.* The Danville, Kentucky, native is a graduate of the University of Kentucky and Spalding University, and Spalding University's MFA in Writing program. He holds honorary doctoral degrees from Transylvania University and the University of Kentucky and is currently the executive director of Kentucky's Governor's School for the Arts and a vice president of the Kentucky Center.